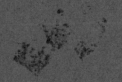

The Curiosity Book

Text by Selma G. Lanes
Illustrated by Robert J. Lee

Platt & Munk, Publishers / New York

A Message from the Author

More than 50 years ago, Rudyard Kipling wrote a story called *The Elephant's Child*. The Elephant's Child "asked questions about everything that he saw, or heard, or felt, or smelt, or touched." Mr. Kipling said of him that he was full of " 'satiable curtiosities." By this he could have meant that, though the elephant's child asked ever so many questions, all the questions he asked had perfectly good answers.

The Curiosity Book also asks ever so many questions, hoping that it provides perfectly good answers to them. The questions are those that students like you really asked.

The author, in fact, here offers her sincere thanks to the principal, Mr. Robert LeBlanc, the teachers (especially Mrs. Kathleen Jones) and the pupils of the lower grades of The Killingworth Elementary School in Killingworth, Connecticut, as well as to her own son, Andrew, and his friends from Public School 6 in New York City, for their help in asking questions. For help in phrasing the answers, thanks go to Catherine R. Allen, whose experience as the eldest in a family of six children proved invaluable.

May *The Curiosity Book* be as useful to readers as a brand-new trunk proved to be for Mr. Kipling's curious Elephant's Child.

S.G.L.

4

What was the world like when it was brand new?

In the beginning, the sun, the earth and the rest of the solar system were only a great dark cloud of dust and gas. Slowly, through thousands of centuries, this dust and gas began to mix together. More and more material was pulled and pushed into a growing ball by the force of gravitation. The ball was squeezed together more and more firmly, until the pressure at the center became so great that gigantic explosions of gases took place, and the sun was born. Some of the dust and gas cloud still spun round the sun and eventually other smaller balls formed. These were the planets and their satellites. The earth is more than four and one-half billion years old. At first, it was only a soft lump of melted minerals and gases. Later a solid crust developed which covered the core of molten hot rock, gases and metal. Only then could soil form and plant life—basic to all other life—develop.

What is the sun?

The sun is a glowing-hot mass of gases, so hot that 4,000,000 tons of itself is turned directly into heat and light each passing second. The temperature on the surface of the sun is more than 10,000 degrees Fahrenheit, and at the center it is more than 30,000,000 degrees Fahrenheit. Two gases—*hydrogen* and *helium*—form 95 per cent of the sun's substance. The sun sends out heat and light by means of a chemical reaction similar to that of the hydrogen bomb: it changes hydrogen into helium. The sun does not burn like a fire, for all fires need oxygen and there is none on the sun. It glows like a gigantic electric light bulb with a heat much hotter than fire. Though the sun loses 240,-000,000 tons in heat and light each minute, it is so big that it won't be used up for billions of years. The sun weighs 331,000 times as much as the earth. If it were an empty shell, 1,300,000 earths could fit inside it. Without its steady heat and light, we could not survive on earth.

How did man discover fire?

According to the Greek legend, man discovered fire only because of the disobedience of Prometheus, one of the lesser gods. Zeus, the ruler of all the gods, did not want man to have fire because it would give human beings too much power. But Prometheus took pity on man. He stole some firebrands from Zeus's hearth and hurled them down to earth.

No one will ever be sure how man first discovered fire, but it was undoubtedly by accident. Lightning may have started a forest fire, or a field of high grass may have burst into flames during a hot summer. Once he overcame his fear, man realized that the heat and light of this new thing—fire—could be of great benefit to him. At first, he probably lit wood torches from an existing fire. Later, when he began to make his own crude tools, he found that when he hammered with rocks, or rubbed sticks and stones, he created sparks. Later still, he discovered that certain substances—like flint—made sparks more easily than others. In comparatively recent times, man learned to make matches, and he could then start fires whenever he liked.

6

When was the first circus?

Men have entertained each other with trained animals, juggling and acrobatics since early times. Those who watched stood or sat in a circle around the performer, so the Latin word *circus,* meaning a ring, came to describe such entertainment. In medieval times, traveling circuses became popular. Troupes of jugglers, acrobats and animals traveled in vans and entertained in castles and towns. The first circus in the United States played in New York and Philadelphia in the 18th century and George Washington is said to have seen it.

Why do the balloon man's balloons go up in the air when the ones children blow up don't?

The balloons that you or your father blow up are filled with air from the lungs. Since this is no lighter than the air around you, such balloons will not rise to the ceiling. The balloon man's balloons are blown up from a tank filled with helium or another gas which is lighter than air. This gas causes his balloons to rise and to float in the air for a long time. Eventually, as you have probably noticed, even the balloon man's balloons come off the ceiling and slowly sink to the floor. That is because no balloon's knot is absolutely leak-proof. Little by little the gas on the inside gets mixed with air from the outside. As this happens, the balloon grows heavier and falls.

What is a marshmallow made of?

Marshmallows look and feel as if they are made of some strange substance, but actually they are made from such ordinary ingredients as egg whites, corn syrup and sugar. The marshmallow got its odd name from the mallow family of plants. The cotton plant is a member of this family. Another plant in the family is actually called the "marshmallow," and once it was used in making candy, though not the kind called marshmallow today.

Why does popcorn pop?

When a kernel of popcorn is heated, its skin bursts open, the way a balloon bursts when you stick a pin in it. The kernels of corn used for popping are small and hard, but they contain moisture. When you heat the kernels, the moisture inside turns to steam. This steam tries to escape from inside the shell, and when the pressure it creates becomes stronger than the skin of the kernel, the skin bursts, the inner meat pushes through the shell and the corn is "popped."

Why do jumping beans jump?

A Mexican jumping bean does not move by itself—what makes it jump is the wriggly *larva* (or fertilized egg) of a small moth growing inside it. The moth lays its eggs in the flower of the bean plant in the spring. A bean pod forms around the egg, and as the egg continues to grow inside the pod, it slowly eats away the meat of the pod. As it does this, it wriggles, making the bean jump. After several months, the insect pierces through the bean pod and comes out a full-grown moth.

Why don't all birds just stay down south?

Birds in the north begin to move south—to *migrate*—only when the food they like to eat grows scarce in cool autumn weather. Birds whose food supply dwindles first are the first to move. Birds who thrive on autumn berries stay longer. In search of food, birds go far enough south to reach a place where food is plentiful for their species. They probably would not return north if that food stayed plentiful. But springtime is the mating season for most birds, and instinct correctly tells them there will no longer be enough food where they are for all the new babies. They begin to fly north with the warm weather in search of newly sprouted greenery for their families. Birds in the southern hemisphere—in countries like Argentina and Australia—migrate northward toward the equator when the weather gets cool. Certain hearty and highly adaptable birds—notably pigeons, sparrows and blue jays—never migrate at all.

8

How did Hallowe'en begin?

Hallowe'en comes from a religious rite celebrated by the ancient Celts of the British Isles. November 1 signaled the beginning of winter and the coming of cold weather (as six months later, May Day heralded the coming of spring). October 31 was the day that herds of livestock were brought in from pasture and bedded down for the winter. The Celts thought that, like animals, the souls of the dead would also like to come in from the cold that day to warm themselves by a cozy fire. They also believed that witches, goblins and fairies came out especially on this night to trap lonely travelers. In time, the old superstitions died out with the Celtic religion. Today Hallowe'en is a children's holiday.

Why am I afraid of the dark?

Man has learned a lot since cavemen first walked the earth. Today we are not afraid of many of the things that frightened our earliest ancestors, such as the setting of the sun, or thunder and lightning. But even today we all fear what we do not know, and so we are sometimes afraid of the dark because we do not know what it may hide. In the light, we can see everything around us. When we are in the dark and cannot see, a small noise or a strange shape can be imagined into a number of scary things. A chair with a shirt hung over it may look like a ferocious bear. Our imaginations replace our eyes at night, and it is no accident that non-existent creatures like witches, ghosts and goblins are almost always "seen" at night. Babies do not imagine that chairs are bears or that there are witches in the shadows, because babies are not grown-up enough to know about such things. Anyone old enough to have a good imagination, even grownups, will be afraid of the dark many times in his life.

What was man's first pet?

Hundreds of thousands of years ago the earliest men lived in caves and had to hunt for food to live. Before man ever arrived on earth, wild dogs lived in much the same way. With his superior intelligence, man devised weapons that made him a better hunter, and dogs began to follow men on their hunting expeditions, to get whatever share they could of the food. The dog's instinct for companionship led him to adopt man as his master. Soon men began to train dogs to help in the hunt, perhaps to carry burdens and to warn of danger. All this happened long before written history, but evidence of it survives, in the bones of primitive dogs found with those of men in Stone Age caves.

When did cats become pets?

Cats were not hunting companions or watchful guardians like dogs, and man did not find a use for them until much later in history. Some cat lovers like to think that it was the beauty of the furry cat that led man to tame it. A more likely reason is that cats were natural enemies of mice and rats. Almost 11,000 years ago, man discovered the secret of planting grain and began to store food from season to season, to use when future crops were bad. Cats could protect these crops and granaries from rats, mice and other small rodents. Probably the cat was first tamed in Egypt. As early as 4,000 years ago, Egyptians had house cats. Ancient Egyptian tombs have drawings of cats, and even cat mummies. For a long time, the ancient Egyptians worshiped cats as gods and goddesses. When a temple cat died, it was mourned by the whole city and its mummy was prepared for burial in the same way as the remains of kings and nobles.

Which are the smartest animals?

Not counting human beings, and leaving out dolphins until scientists make up their minds about them, the ten smartest animals are thought to be the chimpanzee, orangutan, gorilla, monkey, dog, cat, raccoon, elephant, pig and horse. There are animal trainers who will argue that whales, dolphins and elephants are the smartest animals, with human beings fitting in somewhere between whale and elephant. It depends in part on how you measure intelligence. Elephants can learn many commands. Other animals—like beavers—can do remarkably complicated things by instinct but cannot be trained by man. Generally, intelligence in an animal can be roughly measured by the relation of brain size to body size.

Can animals talk to each other?

Though we can hear many sounds insects make, they have no voices. The clicking of certain wood beetles is produced when their heads hit tree stumps. But insects do communicate with one another. One bee tells others where nectar can be found by a precise kind of dance. Ants do much of their "talking" by touch.

The larger animals talk to one another by an exchange of roars, grunts, growls and purrs. Scientists have found at least 20 different sounds chimpanzees make. If you have a cat, you know how much it can tell with a well-timed meow. No animals talk as we do, though parrots in human company can imitate sounds. Dolphins can, too. Recently, scientists working with dolphins, or porpoises, discovered they have a highly developed vocal communication. Dolphins may well turn out to be the smartest of all animals.

Why is the lion "King of Beasts?"

The lion probably received this title because of the way it looks. Male lions have an impressive golden mane that circles a proud head, somewhat like a king's crown. Actually, the lion is not as fierce, powerful or large as some other animals. The Bengal tiger is a more likely candidate for the title "King of Beasts." It has a much heartier appetite than the lion and will attack a wider variety of wild and domestic animals, even man, if hungry enough. In India, about 1,000 persons are killed each year by man-eating tigers.

Are there dragons?

Many thousands of years ago in Babylon, men made pictures of dragons. Later, they often wrote stories about them. The dragon was always a large beast looking like a lizard or serpent. Often it had wings, too. Dragons were usually bad, and the job of heroes was to kill them. One creature on earth that actually looked like a dragon was the *pterodactyl,* a member of the dinosaur family that lived some 70 million years ago. Giant, winged and reptile-like, it died out long before man appeared.

Yet man didn't just imagine dragons. He saw animals that were probably crocodiles, alligators or other reptiles. The largest alligators and crocodiles are more than 20 feet long and certainly could scare—as well as eat—any man. The dragon was common in stories of China, a land where both alligators and crocodiles live. Unlike their western relatives, Chinese dragons were thought to bring good luck. Almost all dragons, east and west, were believed to be capable of breathing fire. The explanation for this could be that crocodiles live in swamps, which often appear to steam as the air above them cools.

Could you dig a hole to China?

The deepest that scientists have been able to dig into the earth with special instruments is 36,198 feet at a spot in the Pacific Ocean. The rock deep inside the earth is much harder than that near the top and is, as yet, impossible to penetrate. Even if scientists could bore through such rock, the tool they used would be melted by the heat at the earth's deeper core.

14

What is color?

To see anything we need light. Light is one of two forms of energy (the other is heat) sent down in invisible waves by the sun. Light waves travel through space in straight lines called rays. Though sunlight has no particular color, we can see, if we look through a special triangular piece of glass called a *prism*, that clear sunlight can be broken up into all the colors of the rainbow: red, orange, yellow, green, blue and violet. This happens because a prism's glass bends light of different wavelengths differently, and every color has a different wavelength. Each wavelength, by itself, produces on the optic nerves in our eye a special stimulation which causes the brain to see one particular color. So it is the separation of light into its different wavelengths that makes us see color. More than a thousand variations or shades of color can be seen by a normal eye.

What makes us see color in clothes or paints?

Light can be separated into its different wavelengths in another way besides the bending of its rays. The special pigments which make us see different colors of paint or crayons or dye for cloth have the ability to absorb all the wavelengths of light, except the one that the eye sees. Black is created when a surface absorbs light of every wavelength, reflecting back no light at all. Black is really the absence of all light.

Why is the sky blue?

The air which surrounds our earth is filled with tiny specks of dust and water vapor. These are of such a size and quality that they scatter more light of the shorter wavelengths—violet, blue and green—than they do of the longer reds and yellows. This scattered or *diffused* light is what we see as blue sky. On the moon, where there is no atmosphere, the light from the sun is white and the sky black.

Because the light of the rising and setting sun passes through more dust particles, the colors with longer wavelengths are scattered as well, and more colors become visible.

After a rainstorm, there may be millions of tiny raindrops still left in the air when the sun comes out. These drops can act like prisms, separating sunlight into its individual colors. What we see then is a rainbow.

What is sound?

Sound is made by a rapid back and forth movement in the air called a *vibration*. Vibrations travel in a wave pattern. The sound of a bee buzzing is caused by the incredibly fast movements of its wings, which make the air vibrate. When a person talks, two vocal cords in his throat vibrate and make airwaves. We hear sound when such vibrations strike our eardrums. The eardrum, composed of a thin layer of tightly drawn skin, receives vibrations from the air and passes them on to the brain, where they become "sounds." If you want to test sound as vibrations, try striking a metal gong or a tuning fork. The sound will end as soon as the touch of your finger on the metal stops the vibrations.

What was the first musical instrument?

All primitive peoples had musical instruments of the drum family. The beats of the drum were like a language and could carry messages over distances the voice could not reach. The American Indians, among many others, used the drum as a kind of telephone. Early man also soon discovered that he could make noise by blowing through the horns of animals. These horns were the ancestors of today's brass band instruments. Reed instruments made of various grasses held between the thumbs or palms of the hand, and later inserted in hollowed-out sticks, probably came next. These were the earliest instruments on which man could make real music, for different notes could be blown and tone could be controlled. The stringed instruments came last, starting with ones that man plucked with his fingers, like the harp. Later stringed instruments were played with a bow.

Why does the sound of the sea stay in a seashell?

Though it is pleasant to think that the sounds we hear when we hold a seashell up to the ear are those of the ocean's waves, they are not. They are really sounds from the air waves around us, wherever we happen to be. Some seashells are so made that they are able to pick up sounds from the air and make them stronger. Scientists call these shells *resonators*. A good resonator will pick up many sounds the human ear cannot normally hear and magnify them. This is what the seashell does when you put it to your ear in what you think is a perfectly quiet place.

Why can't people fly?

The only animals who can fly are those with wings, and winged flight is so complex that a bird weighing more than 40 pounds can't fly. Flying requires the ability to overcome the pull of gravity. This is possible only when the flow of air on the underside of a bird—or plane or other object—is strong enough to lift it off the earth. If a bird's weight is twice another's, its wings have to be four times as strong for it to take off and fly. A flying bird's muscles make up more than half its weight. It is easy to see that a bird the size of a man would need enormous wing power. Leonardo da Vinci long ago dreamed of designing wings for a man, and while that dream has really never died, it has never come true, either. Large airplanes can take off in spite of weights up to 550,000 pounds only because of their powerful engines, which give them the "muscle power" to overcome gravity.

How did the man who made the first clock know what time it was?

The clock was invented in the 14th century and has changed little since the 18th century. Clocks are just one convenient way of measuring time. Man could tell time long before the clock came along. Cavemen knew that daylight was followed by about the same interval of darkness. They were soon able to divide the daylight hours into parts by noticing the different shadows cast on trees or upright sticks by the sun as it moved across the sky. Early in history, men divided daylight into morning and afternoon. The New Testament speaks of a 12-hour day, and the Romans are given credit for establishing a 24-hour period for a night and a day. Before the present-day clock was invented, men commonly used waterclocks. These measured time by letting water escape slowly from a container with a small hole. A man could tell how much time had passed by seeing how much water remained in the container. Later, this principle was used in hour and minute glasses which had sand running between two glass bulbs. By the time a man named De Vick constructed the first mechanical clock in 1364, he and everyone else knew how to measure the passing of time.

Why is it a different time of day in California than in New York?

As the earth turns, the sun moves across the sky toward the west. This means that sunrise always comes later to the people who live west of you, and earlier to those living east. The United States is so wide—some 3,000 miles from New York to California—that it is divided into four different time zones. These zones are based on the hour that the sun rises in different parts of the country. Sunrise in San Francisco comes three hours later than in New York City.

Where did yesterday go?

Time is something you cannot see, hear, taste, smell or touch. But you can measure and remember it. You may have learned something new in school yesterday, or made a new friend. All of history written in books is a remembering of yesterdays, and, of course, the years of a person's life are comprised of many yesterdays. What yesterday means simply is that 24 hours of time passed, a passage of time that can be measured on a clock. There is only one place on earth where, for a short while, a person can go back into yesterday. In the middle of the Pacific Ocean, there is an imaginary line called the international date line which runs from the North to the South Pole. If you are crossing the ocean from Japan to California on a Monday, when you pass that imaginary line you will move from Monday back to Sunday. That happens because the international date line is, by agreement, the point at which one day ends and the next begins. It is the only place you can ever catch up with yesterday.

18

Marine Iguana, Galapagos Island

What are living things made of?

Every plant and animal alive is made up of cells. These are tiny blobs of living matter that come in many different shapes, and they can be seen only under a microscope. Every cell has two parts: an outer sphere of a jelly-like substance called *protoplasm* and, inside this protoplasm, a more solid center called the *nucleus*. A human body contains about 60 trillion cells, and each of these cells can divide itself and produce new cells. In this way, old cells are constantly being replaced by new ones. This process is what keeps us alive.

Our first living ancestor was a single cell floating in the stormy oceans of the earth about two billion years ago. This cell had an ability to reproduce itself. It probably came into existence as a result of the violent electrical storms and extreme heat of the sun bombarding the earth during its first half-billion-year infancy. The heat and electricity combined to rearrange some of the earth's gases into acids capable of forming this first cell. From this cell, over thousands of centuries, evolved all living things on our planet.

What was the first animal that still exists on earth?

The horseshoe crab is one of the earliest forms of sea life still in existence. It is more than 400 million years old. The scorpion, the first known land animal, is about 300 million years old. Neither of these creatures is as old as a marine animal called a sponge. The sponge is nearly one billion years old, one of the oldest and lowest forms of animal life. While most animals have changed greatly over millions of years, certain reptiles and lizards —like the iguana of the Americas and the Pacific—look much the same today as their ancestors did millions of years ago.

What animal lives the longest?

The giant tortoise of the Galapagos Islands has the longest life of any animal. It can live to be 200 years old. It is more than four feet in length and can weigh 600 pounds. Easily caught by human beings, it is now almost extinct.

Can a porcupine shoot its quills?

The porcupine is a fat, blunt-nosed animal with almost no neck and a short, wide tail. The fur on its underside and face is soft, but from the top of its head to its tail, the fur is peppered with sharp, pointed quills. Often called a "quill pig," a full-grown porcupine has hundreds of quills. These vary in length from one inch on its head to six inches or more on its back. When a porcupine is attacked, it puts its head down and arches its back like a cat, making its quills stand up. The porcupine can lash out with its bristling tail. The quills are easily detached from the porcupine's skin, particularly when it shakes its tail, but it cannot actually shoot them. The quills have sharp barbed points and if they become lodged in the skin of another animal, they work themselves in deeper and deeper and can even kill a victim. The porcupine can be a dangerous foe, until it is turned on its back. Then it becomes quite helpless.

How do fish breathe?

Fish do not breathe in air through lungs as human beings and other animals do. Instead they have gills which remove oxygen from the water. A fish drowns on land because it can get oxygen only by taking water in through the mouth. This water flows over the fish's gills and out again, through openings behind the covers of the gills, leaving its oxygen behind. There are exceptions. The *climbing perch* has gills that let it breathe air for some time, and it can walk on land using movable spines on its gill covers. The African *lungfish* has a primitive lung-like air bladder, and during summer dry spells it can burrow in the mud and sleep for months out of water.

What is water?

Water is a combination—or *compound*—of two gases. It consists of two atoms of a light gas, *hydrogen,* and one atom of a heavier gas, *oxygen*. Water is formed when hydrogen is burned in oxygen, causing the gases to become a liquid. Almost 90 per cent of the weight of water is oxygen. The earth's surface is more than 70 per cent water. This water was made during the earth's first two to three billion years as it cooled down. At some point, the earth reached the right temperature for great quantities of its hydrogen gas to burn in oxygen. In a science class, you can produce small amounts of water by combining the two gases, hydrogen and oxygen. Water exists in one of three forms: as a liquid; as a solid, ice; or as a gas called water vapor.

Does the air we breathe get used up?

Every time each of us takes in a breath, we are using up some of the oxygen in our atmosphere and replacing it with another gas, *carbon dioxide*. But other living things replace the oxygen we use. In the exact reverse of what human beings and other animals do, green plants take in carbon dioxide and give out oxygen through their leaves. (Plants need carbon dioxide from the air and water from the soil to make their own food, a sugar called *glucose*.) In this way, nature maintains a steady supply of these two vital gases.

Why don't we use up the earth's water?

We use the earth's water all the time. When a farmer grows wheat, it takes approximately a ton of water to produce each pound. Yet, just as quickly as living things use up moisture, it is being returned to the atmosphere. The roots of plants take water from the soil and pass it on to the leaves. Much of this water returns to the air through the pores of a plant's leaves. On a warm, breezy day, a good-sized tree will return many gallons of moisture to the atmosphere. The sun constantly draws moisture into the air from from the soil, rivers and oceans, and from animal life. Eventually, this moisture returns to the earth as rain.

22

Are owls really wise?

Owls are no more intelligent than other birds. The owl probably got a reputation for wisdom because it looks like a professor, with its great, staring eyes, always questioning "whoo? whoo?" and its dignified, fluffy plumage—like a solemn professor's academic gown.

What is imagination?

Imagination is thinking beyond things we have actually seen or experienced. Since we can only think about what we know, imagination and imaginary creatures all have some part of reality in them. When you pretend with your friends that you are cowboys or soldiers or animals or grownups, all these things that you think of are made up of things that you know. Although you may never have seen a real cowboy or soldier, you can imagine how they look and behave from books you have read and pictures you have seen. Even homework, which seems more like work than play, includes imagination. When you read about ancient people and great heroes, you can almost picture what they looked like. This is imagination. When you need to find your way out of a bad situation, you think of all the possibilities and imagination helps you. When you dream or have nightmares, your imagination is also at work.

How do plants and trees eat?

Flowers, plants and trees eat by taking in minerals and water from the soil through their roots. They also take in carbon dioxide from the air through their leaves. But this nourishment would be of little use to them were it not for a chemical in the leaves and stems of all green plants called *chlorophyll*. Chlorophyll enables plants to turn minerals, water and gas into usable food. Chlorophyll needs sunshine in order to use its miraculous powers on the food of trees and plants. By a process known as *photosynthesis,* chlorophyll makes the plants' living tissue able to absorb the sun's energy—its heat and light—and change it into life-nourishing plant food.

How do leaves change color in autumn?

Tree leaves turn from green to yellow or red and then to brown when the soil dries at the end of summer and cooler weather comes. Then the tree cannot draw as much moisture as it needs up into its leaves. This lack of moisture causes the chlorophyll—a green chemical—in its leaves to break down and disappear. The other pigments in the leaf then become visible, and the leaves turn to the shades of red, yellow and brown that make early autumn the gayest season of the year.

Why don't pine trees lose their needles in winter?

Evergreens do not shed their leaves when winter comes because they do not lose their moisture supply in winter as other trees do. Many evergreens have a central root, called a tap root, which goes much deeper into the ground than the roots of other trees. This lets them take in moisture and minerals from the soil long after earth close to the top has hardened and frozen. Then too, the long tubular needles of evergreens hold moisture much better and for much longer than other, flatter leaves. With their steady supply of moisture, evergreen leaves often remain on the tree for two to five years and sometimes for as long as 20 years.

Why do we have to eat vegetables?

Vegetables are parts of plants: leaves (like lettuce), seeds (beans and corn), and roots (carrots). Since plants make their own food, glucose, and absorb many minerals from the soil, vegetables are rich in nutrition. The glucose itself is easily used by our body cells for energy. From meat, fish and eggs, we get protein, fats, and minerals such as calcium and iron. But we also need those minerals and vitamins that only vegetables can provide. Vitamin B_2 from leafy vegetables helps the body's cells to use oxygen from the air. Vitamin B_1 helps the body to digest and use food. The Vitamin C in tomatoes and citrus fruits helps to build stronger gums. Raw vegetables are even better for us than cooked ones, since cooking and draining often remove valuable vitamins.

Why do I get tired?

You get tired because the organs and tissues of your body work hard while you are awake. Many separate nerve messages pass between the brain and an arm or leg when you walk or raise and lower a spoon. After a day of such work, your brain and muscles begin to signal that they need rest. Your muscles may begin to ache. The nerve messages move more slowly and the brain tells the body it is time to slow down. One theory to explain why all this happens is that each movement we make results in damaged cells in our body, and these cells accumulate in the blood stream. When enough of such cells are deposited there, our blood undergoes a change which causes fatigue and we must rest so that these damaged cells can be repaired or replaced.

Why do some things hurt me?

You feel pain when the nerves send a message from some part of the body to the brain. The message says that something out of the ordinary has happened. The nerves are living fibers that transmit chemical messages to the brain. When we cut a finger, it is not really the finger that hurts. What causes our feeling of pain is the shock the brain receives when the nerves of a finger let it know that some injury has occurred. You can test the truth of this the next time you visit the dentist. Before he begins to work on your aching tooth, the dentist will probably give you an *anesthetic* to numb the nerves around the tooth and stop them from sending out a pain message to the brain. Under anesthesia your aching tooth will stop hurting.

Where do tears come from?

There are tears in your eyes even when you aren't crying. While your eyes are open, a small tear gland at the outer corner of each eye produces tears every six seconds. Every time you blink your eyelids, these tears are pumped out of your tear glands and into your eyes. They keep the surface of your eyes moist and clear off small particles of dust and other impurities from the air. The same thing happens, in an exaggerated way, when you cry. If you are sad or happy, the tension you feel at such times sometimes acts on the facial muscles, and the muscles near the eye squeeze your tear glands. Tears then begin to flow freely. Similarly, when you laugh very hard, the facial muscles press on the tear glands and tears may stream out of your eyes.

How do bees sting?

Most female bees have a sting which helps them to protect the hive from enemies. This defense weapon is often turned against man. The sting is a needle-like extension which can be thrust from between the two end parts of a bee's abdomen. Because a sting is usually hooked at the end, it may remain in the flesh. If you scrape off this stinger quickly, the bite will be less painful. When the stinger remains in your flesh, it often pulls soft parts of the bee's body with it. In such cases, the bee will die. The queen bee can use her sting over and over again, but she uses it only against other queens.

How do bees make honey?

The honeybee visits a flower and sips the nectar with its tongue. The nectar is then swallowed and deposited in a honey sac, a stomach-like bag just in front of the bee's regular stomach. A valve connects the two pouches so that a hungry bee can eat some of the nectar itself. While the nectar is in the honey sac, it is acted upon by juices from the bee's glands. These juices change the sugar of the nectar chemically so that it turns into honey. When the bee gets to the hive, it can suck back the nectar from the honey sac and deposit it in the cells of the comb. Honeybees do this by instinct, just as they form colonies by instinct. In fact, honeybees die if they are forced to live alone.

How do spiders spin webs?

The silky thread which spiders use in making webs comes from tiny openings at the tip of their abdomen. The thread comes out from special glands as a liquid, and turns into a solid as it mixes with air. Spiders have three pairs of spinning organs called *spinnerets,* which combine the solid threads into various thicknesses. Spiders can make a sticky silk thread to catch bugs, a stronger strand to support the web, and a special, fluffy thread on which to lay eggs. Certain spiders spin no webs but live on a leaf or bit of bark. The spider is not an insect, but belongs to a special group of eight-legged creatures called *arachnids.*

What makes flowers smell?

Flowers smell because of the oils in their petals. These oils are produced as the plant grows. When the flower blooms, the oil in the petals often decomposes, and as it evaporates, it gives that flower its own distinctive smell. Not all plants give off lovely perfume. Skunk cabbage has an unpleasant "skunky" smell, and the giant calla lilly, which may be eight and one-half feet tall, smells like decaying meat.

How do new flowers grow?

Flowers grow from seeds, and two things are necessary for a seed to form. Inside the blossom of every flower there are tiny eggs (the female cells) and also *pollen* (the male cells). These are almost always present in one flower. But pollen can seldom drop by itself near the egg of its own blossom. The pollen must be carried by the wind, or on the legs and bodies of insects, from one blossom to another. In this way, the pollen of one blossom will reach the egg of another. When it does, that egg becomes a fertilized seed. The seed then falls to the ground to become the next year's new flowering plant. Some plants produce very few seeds, while certain trees drop thousands of seeds.

Where do baby fish come from?

A mother fish may lay millions of tiny eggs (female cells) in a single mating season. She usually does this in a shallow nest on the sandy bottom of an ocean or a lake, not too far from shore. When this happens, a father fish will pour sperm (male cells) over the eggs. Both the mother's eggs and the father's sperm come from an opening on the underside of their bodies, close to the tail. Those eggs not reached by sperm will not become fish. Many eggs that are fertilized by the sperm will be eaten and destroyed by other fish. Many of the thousands of baby fish who develop from these eggs will also be eaten and destroyed.

Where do baby birds come from?

A mother bird produces a number of eggs inside her body. The father bird will fly onto the mother bird's back in such a way that his male cells of reproduction—the *sperm*—will be released into a passage in the mother bird that leads to where the eggs are stored. After a hard protective shell has formed over her eggs, the mother bird lays them. She and the father bird usually take turns sitting on the fertilized eggs to keep them warm. The baby birds grow inside the shell, and in a few weeks break it open.

Where do I come from?

Each living species has the ability to reproduce itself. In all mammals, including human beings, the fertilization of the egg and its growth from egg to fully-developed young take place inside the mother. All mammals carry their young inside them for various lengths of time until they are ready to be born. Rabbits may have four or five litters of young in a single year. An elephant produces one baby in a period of 22 months. Human beings have babies in nine months. Human children are conceived when the sperm cell from a father unites with an egg cell from a mother. This union takes place inside the mother's body. When sperm and egg cell join, they form a new single cell which divides and redivides in a pattern unique to the human species. At the end of nine months of cell division and growth, a new human baby is born.

How do we grow?

The growth of cells is what controls the growth of plants, animals or human beings. In human beings, the rate of cell growth until we reach maturity at the age of about 22 is controlled by a system of glands called the *endocrine glands*. These glands are located in four places: the base of the skull, the neck, the chest and the sexual organs. A newborn infant's cells grow faster during the first weeks of life than they ever will again. The process of cell growth then slows down, but speeds up again, usually between the ages of ten and 12 for girls, and 12 and 14 for boys. Even after the body reaches full growth, however, cell division and growth continue. Certain cells die and others take their place. When an arm or leg is bruised, new cells form—by division—to take the place of those destroyed. Broken bones mend themselves the same way.

Why do we get old and die?

Stones and metals do not die because they are not made of living matter. We grow old and die because we are alive. At some point, after we are fully grown, our cells no longer divide as quickly, nor can our bodies replace all of the cells that die. With great age, our bodies slow down and even shrink, as our cells wear down and finally lose life, not to be replaced by new cells.

Once we are alive, however, we are forever part of the life chain of our species, our planet and the universe. Though human beings die, they live on in their children and in the record of their lives and works.

What makes people different colors?

Anthropologists agree that all of mankind goes back to the same prehistoric ancestors. They believe that all racial differences—of color, size, shape and physical features—represent ways in which men became successful at surviving under special conditions in different areas of the earth. Every human being has the same four color pigments in his skin—red, yellow, white and black. Which of these colors he is depends on the proportion of the four pigments in his skin. In the lands near the equator, where dark-skinned people originated, the sun is very strong. Ultraviolet rays from the sun would cause the body to produce too much Vitamin D. Therefore, the skin produces a great deal of the brown pigment, *melanin,* which blocks the ultraviolet rays. In cooler climates, where the sun does not shine so directly, this protection is not needed. In fact, the skin must be able to absorb large quantities of sun to produce enough Vitamin D for health. The smaller amounts of melanin give the skin a lighter color. Man's need to adapt to a given area seems to be what finally determined skin color.

What are freckles?

Our skin is composed of many different layers of cells and these cells do different things. In the top layer of the skin there are special kinds of cells called *melanocytes* which produce the brownish pigment that gives skin color. The more skin is exposed to the sun, the more brown pigment is produced. When melanocytes are in perfect working order, the color is spread evenly over the skin—becoming a suntan. In many people, however, the melanocytes work unevenly and freckles result.

Why is some hair curly and other hair straight?

Like so many other physical characteristics—the shape of your head, the color of your eyes—the kind of hair you have depends on genes you inherited from your parents. Most peoples of European origin have hair that is mildly wavy and smooth, varying in color from black through blond. Seen under a microscope, this type of hair appears quite oval in shape at its end. In contrast, the people of China and the American Indians have hair that is perfectly straight and almost always black. Examined at one of its ends, it will look perfectly round. Such hair tends to be heavier and coarser than other types. Almost all the dark-skinned races and the natives of Australia have hair that is curly. A very frizzy, curly hair appears quite flat under a microscope.

What makes different people like different things?

No two persons on earth are exactly alike. From our parents we get microscopic units of inheritance called *genes*, which never combine in exactly the same way in any two people, even in brothers and sisters. These genes make each person unique, with a physical make-up no other person has. Being different, we will respond differently. We may inherit particularly sensitive rods and cones in the retinas of our eyes, and these will make us respond to certain colors in a special way. One person may have particularly keen taste buds on the top of his tongue. He will be sensitive to sweet and salty things. Another may have keener taste buds at the sides of his tongue. He will be more aware of sour foods. Then, too, we grow up in homes with different customs and needs. Eskimos eat blubber—whale fat—because it keeps them warm in the frigid north. We all have individual and social experiences that affect us in different ways. Two people will never like or dislike all the same things.

Why does the alphabet go A B C?

Our alphabet is based on the Roman alphabet, which developed 2,500 years ago from the first known alphabet of sound signs. This was created about 1,000 years earlier by a Semitic people who lived on the eastern shore of the Mediterranean Sea.

Before this discovery, man wrote with pictures. If earliest man drew a group of animals, this might mean he had found a good place to hunt. Soon these pictures began to represent ideas, too. A drawing of a deer, for example, could represent a deer and also the idea of running. This was called an *ideograph*. The Egyptian hieroglyphics were ideographic writing. Ideographs let man tell more in his picture-writing, but different men could read a message different ways. Gradually, pictures came to represent sounds. If the word for sun were "ra," then a picture of the sun represented the sound "ra." This was *syllabic* writing.

An alphabet of sound signs was far more efficient than ideographs or syllabic writing. In such an alphabet a limited number of signs served for all the usual sounds human beings make. Both the Hebrews and the Phoenicians adopted this basic sound alphabet. The Phoenicians carried their alphabet to Greece, and the Romans later modified the Greek alphabet.

Did children always go to school?

Children have always learned lessons. But for a long time, their only school was everyday life, and they learned by watching what grown-ups around them did. In many parts of the world this is still true. It is only in advanced civilizations that formal schools have come into existence. A school is a place where groups of children (or grownups) can come together for the purpose of organized learning. Our present schools have grown from the first schools of the ancient Greeks. These began with great thinkers like Plato and Aristotle traveling from town to town, teaching single pupils and, later, small groups for brief periods. Before long, these Greek teachers realized it would be better to stay in one place and have pupils come to them. The earliest Greek schools were for those who had the leisure to devote to the pure exercise of their minds. It was not until the 18th century that parents and educators began to appreciate how complicated the world was becoming and how practical it was for anyone—rich or poor—to be schooled so that he could understand this world and develop his mind to its fullest capacity.

Indus Seal, about 2300 B.C.

Why do men wear pants and women skirts?

Pants and skirts had their start with the loincloth tied round the waist and the animal skin draped from the shoulder. People of most early civilizations, the Egyptians, for example, dressed in a kind of loincloth which, over the years, became a shorter or longer skirt. In biblical times, men as well as women wore either longish loincloths or skirted tunics draped from the shoulder. Ancient Persian men were probably the first to wear a garment recognizable as pants as an addition to the coat or tunic. These Persian pants were tight at the ankle and gave warriors and horsemen more freedom of movement. Active men in other places soon adopted the improvement. Women spent their time in less strenuous pursuits than men, and they remained in the skirt. Today women, too, wear pants at times, particularly for activities in which freedom of movement is important.

Who wore the first socks?

The first "socks," short and knitted, were worn by Egyptians and Etruscans in the fifth century A.D. These socks were very much like ours today, except they had a separate space for the big toe; thus they were like a mitten for the foot. The Egyptians knitted other things like caps, gloves, and high stockings with fancy patterns. But knitting by hand required much time, and knitted stockings did not become popular until after the knitting machine was invented in England in 1589.

Why do people shake hands?

The handshake began thousands of years ago, as a sign of peace. Long ago, most men lived in the forests. They never knew when they might meet an enemy, animal or human, and so they always carried weapons. If a man met someone he did not know, he had to decide in some way whether the stranger was friend or foe. One of the two would extend his weapon arm, empty-handed, to show that he did not mean to fight. If the other did the same, they would advance and meet in a handclasp. In the beginning, this handclasp may have been simply to prevent either man from changing his mind and reaching for his weapon. In time, it came to be a greeting of friendship.

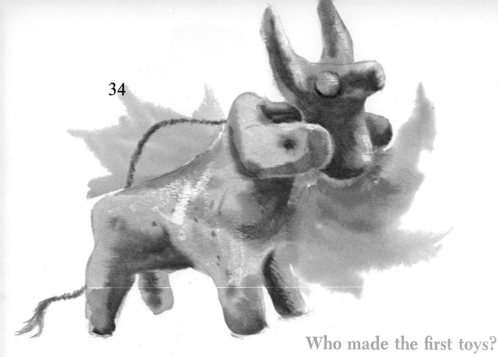

34

*Pre-Columbian Toy Animal
with Movable Head*

Who made the first toys?

Children in prehistoric times played with a rock or a piece of wood when their fathers and mothers were busy. These objects were the first toys, "invented" by children themselves in their need to amuse themselves, as well as to learn. Responding to these needs, parents long ago made their children things more like the toys of today: smaller versions of farm animals, tools and furnishings, such as cradles, tables and chairs. These were real toys, because they were made specially for a child's play.

Why does a ball bounce?

Two things make a ball bounce. One is its *elasticity*. The other is its roundness. Balls are usually made of a material like rubber which has the ability to stretch and then to snap back to its original shape and size, the way a rubber band does. Because a ball is round, it hits the ground at one point and flattens at that spot. It then goes back to its original condition, that of being round. The elastic force is concentrated at the bouncing point, and this force is strong enough to make the ball push back off the ground, or bounce. A square object made of elastic material will not bounce the way a ball does because much more of its surface hits the ground. Because the elastic force is spread out over this surface instead of being concentrated at a single point, it is not powerful enough to make the square push back off the ground.

Who invented the bicycle?

The first really practical bicycle was built in 1839 by a Scotsman, Kirkpatrick MacMillan. There had been similar inventions before it, but most lacked some essential element of the modern bicycle. Earlier models had to be walked along, with the rider's feet pushing against the ground.

Did people ever have tails?

Neither apes nor men have tails, though some remote and unknown ancestor of both—sometimes called the missing link—possibly had one. What apes and men have in common, setting them apart from all other animals, is the ability to stand and walk in an upright position rather than on all fours. They also have a similar brain structure and an appendix in the lower right abdomen. This appendix is an outgrowth of the large intestine and may be the last trace of what was once a tail in a creature related to men and apes.

Why do we need fingernails?

Fingernails are made of a tough form of protein called *keratin*. They are an inheritance from the days when animals walked on all fours and used this finger or toe covering to scratch the ground, to climb trees, to attack and protect themselves from enemies. Even today, man uses his nails: they make his fingers and toes stronger, protecting the skin underneath from damage. And if you've ever had an itch, you know how useful a fingernail can be.

Why do trains need tracks?

Steel tracks make it possible for the wheels of a train to turn very fast without sinking into the ground under the great weight of the engine and its big, bulky cars. Tracks are laid out so that trains will not have to climb high hills, go over big bumps or round any sharp curves.

What is electricity?

You have probably run a hard rubber comb through your hair and heard your hair crackle or seen it stand on end. Or you may have rubbed your feet along a rug and felt a slight shock when you touched a friend's hand. These are forms of static electricity, made by rubbing two different surfaces together: comb and hair, shoes and rug.

All matter is made up of tiny particles that carry a charge, either positive (+) or negative (−). In most things the number of positive and negative charges is equal. It is only when a material has more of one charge or the other that electricity is created. Once made, electricity can travel from one place to another along a conductor such as wiring. When you plug in a toaster, electricity created by a generator at your local power company flows along the toaster wire into the appliance. Electricity can also be made by different combinations of chemicals, as in a car battery.

What causes storms?

Storms begin in places where cold, dry masses of air meet warm, wet masses of air. Usually spearheads of the warmer air pierce the cold. Storms develop at such small points because the cold air whirls in around the warm spot of lighter air, often causing high winds. Vast whirlpools of air, circling over hundreds of miles, can result from such a collision of warm and cool air.

A hurricane is a storm that always starts in warm places over oceans. Hurricanes occur most often in the late summer and early fall when the tropical air is likely to be warmest and have the most moisture. When it meets cold, dry polar air moving toward it, there is a great contrast in temperature between the two air masses. This causes winds, with speeds as high as 190 miles an hour, extending over an area of 300 to 600 miles.

What causes lightning?

The atmosphere always contains electricity. Near the earth, the atmosphere's electricity is negatively charged. The upper atmosphere, for reasons not entirely understood, seems to carry a higher, positive charge of electricity. Certain rainstorms have tall, moisture-laden clouds whose bottoms are close to the ground and whose tops reach as high as five miles into the sky. As the storm starts, small positively charged raindrops from the top of the cloud come in contact with larger negatively charged raindrops forming lower down. The electrically charged drops attract one another and eventually a spark may jump from the top to the bottom of a cloud, from one cloud to another, or between a low cloud and the earth.

Lightning is actually a large flash of electricity. It is jagged because it follows the line of least resistance down to the earth. Warm wet air is a good conductor of electricity, and so each flash takes the warmest, rainiest path downward.

What is thunder?

Thunder is the sound wave that occurs all along the column of air that lightning travels through. The great release of electrical energy in lightning causes vibrations which produce this sound. We hear one sharp clap of thunder if the lightning is nearby. If the electrical storm is some distance away, the thunder sounds more like a rumbling, because the sound comes to us at intervals, from different points along the column of air. Unless an electrical storm is directly overhead, we will hear the thunder some time after we see lightning. This is because light travels 186,000 miles a second and sound only 1,100 feet a second.

Where do rain and snow come from?

Rain, snow, sleet and hail are all forms of condensed water vapor—moisture—which falls from clouds. Moisture evaporates from the earth's surface, from lakes, oceans, trees and land. Clouds are made when warm air filled with moisture rises up into the atmosphere. When it meets cooler air at a certain height, the warm air begins to cool and can no longer hold moisture as water vapor. This extra moisture changes into tiny droplets of water or ice which form a cloud.

When large masses of cold and warm air meet, they mix less violently than small amounts do. The lighter warm air rises up over the cold air in gradual steps, and cools as it does. Clouds of water vapor form and condense into water. The result is either rain or snow, depending upon the temperature and season. You may have heard the weatherman refer to this fall of moisture from the air as *precipitation*.

How does the weatherman know what it will be like tomorrow?

Air has mass and presses down on the earth. Warm air is lighter than cold air, so different pressures are created in the atmosphere as warm air rises to various levels over land and sea. A weatherman charts these different pressure areas. A low-pressure area indicates approaching bad weather, because it means that cold air will be moving in to replace rising warm air that is filled with moisture. When the clouds contain more moisture than they can hold, rain or snow results. A high-pressure area indicates that the weather will be fair, for this means that the air is in a state of balance, its higher and lower levels close to the same temperature. Because the weatherman has made a study of the way in which masses of cold and warm air move in the part of the country where he works, he can often be quite accurate in predicting when a storm will come or go. But sometimes high and low-pressure areas change very rapidly or unpredictably, and then everyone, including the weatherman, may be fooled.

Why do we have winter, spring, summer and autumn?

If the earth's axis were not tilted, the weather would stay the same in a given place all the time. There would be no seasons. Because the earth rotates around its own tipped axis, as well as around the sun, the northern and southern hemispheres receive different amounts of sunlight at a given time. When it is summer in the United States, it is winter in Australia, and vice versa. People who live close to the equator experience less seasonal change because the tilt of the earth's axis affects the middle regions of the earth much less than it does the extremes of north and south.

What is the coldest spot on earth?

Because of the way the earth's axis tilts, the South Pole gets less of the sun's heat than the North Pole, and this makes it colder. In August 1958, at Vostok, Antarctica, a temperature of minus 125.3 degrees Fahrenheit was registered, the lowest on record. Since the South Pole gets less sunlight, it also has a higher concentration of ice and polar winds.

Why is the snow white?

Since clear water and ice can be seen through, you might suppose that a snowflake would be transparent, too. But ice and snow are not the same thing. Ice is frozen water and snow is frozen water vapor. When water vapor freezes, it turns into a crystal with a great many reflecting surfaces. This crystal, or snowflake, reflects back practically all of the sunlight which strikes it, rather than letting it pass through. The reflection of all this light produces the sensation of white to our eyes. Once on the ground, the snowflake is even whiter, because many crystals together reflect back even more light.

Are there any places on earth no one has seen?

There are few places left on earth that civilized man has not explored or seen. On rare occasions, an explorer will stumble upon a tribe deep in the jungle that no one knew was there. But entire continents are no longer a mystery, as the American continents were in the 16th century, Africa in the 19th and the Antarctic well into the 20th. Explorers today have turned their curiosity to the sea, to the interior of the earth and to the stars. Little is now known about the ocean's depths or the inner layers of the earth's crust. And, of course, our greatest curiosity now is fixed on what is in space, on the moon and other planetary bodies.

What is the equator?

The equator is an imaginary line, midway between the North and South Poles, which divides the earth into two halves. The area that extends 23½ degrees of latitude north and south of this imaginary line is called the Tropic Zone. In this area the sun's rays strike the earth vertically, giving more heat than any place else on earth. The 23½-degree band is equal to the angle at which the earth's axis tilts from the vertical. In other words, a line passing through the North and the South Pole is inclined at a 23½-degree angle. This brings the Tropic Zone nearest the sun.

Where is the hottest place in the world?

The highest known temperature, 136 degrees Fahrenheit in the shade, was recorded at Aziza, Libya, in September, 1922. In the sun it was between 30 and 40 degrees hotter. The sun not only provides more heat to countries like Libya, near the equator, but radiation from the desert sand reflects back much of the heat to the surrounding atmosphere.

What was the first plant?

Close to two billion years ago, the first primitive plants formed in the sea. They were soft and jelly-like single cells. These earliest water plants are called *algae*. They do not have roots and absorb food from the water. When algae reach a certain size, they simply divide, one cell becoming two, two becoming four and so on. You can see algae as a green coating on the surface of still water. Land plants developed many millions of years after algae.

Why aren't there dinosaurs any more?

Dinosaurs lived on earth for about 100 million years. During this time, summers became hotter and winters colder, and certain plants that some dinosaurs depended on for food no longer could grow. With less food to eat, these plant-eating dinosaurs could not survive. This meant that meat-eating dinosaurs also had less food, because some of them ate the plant-eating dinosaurs. And dinosaurs, being cold-blooded members of the reptile family, did not thrive in cold weather. As the temperature dropped, they became sleepy and slow. Newer mammals, who were warm-blooded, got more food. They had much bigger brains in proportion to their size than dinosaurs and probably outwitted them in summer as well as winter. Over many millions of years, for these reasons and for others we shall probably never know, the dinosaur disappeared from the earth. The biggest dinosaur that ever lived was the *brachiosaurus*. It weighed about 100,000 pounds and was 80 feet from head to tail.

Why do whales spout?

The ancestor of the whale was a land animal. It took millions of years for the body of this mammal to adapt to life in the water. Like other mammals, whales breathe through their lungs, not through gills as fish do. Millions of years ago, when its ancestors lived on land, a whale's nostrils were probably in the front part of its head, like ours. These nostrils gradually moved to the top of its head and became the one or two blow-holes that enable the whale to breathe at the surface of the ocean. When a whale submerges, its blow-holes are closed by little valves, and so are the air passages from its mouth to its lungs, so that it will not take water in. Whales can stay under water for up to three-quarters of an hour, but they usually come up to breathe about every ten minutes. When they reach the surface, they "blow" or exhale the used air from their lungs with a loud noise. The spout they send up is not water, but used air mixed with water vapor. The whale will blow a number of times, until all the air has been changed and its lungs are filled with fresh air. Then it usually takes a deep dive called "sounding." Whales can dive as deep as 2,000 feet—about three times as deep as an atomic-powered submarine can go.

What is the biggest animal in the world?

The blue whale is the largest animal the world has ever known. It can be more than 100 feet long, and one of the biggest ever caught weighed 130 tons—as much as 1,600 men. The biggest dinosaur of prehistoric times wasn't even half the bulk of the blue whale.

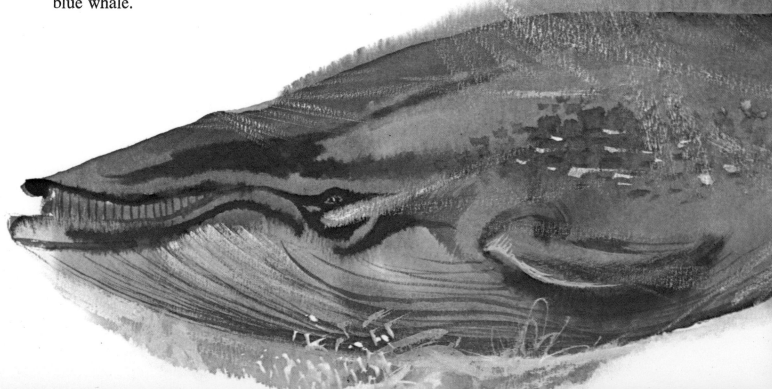

Why does the elephant have a trunk?

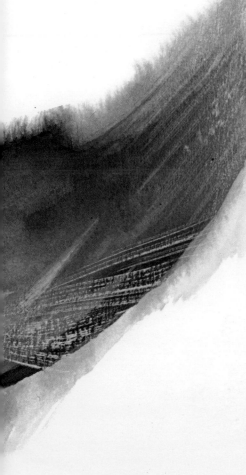

The elephant is the last living relative of giant mammals, often called *mammoths,* which lived after dinosaurs and on through the early days of man. The mammoth was not an efficient animal. Its legs had to carry enormous weight—two and three times the weight of today's elephant—and they were short and fat, useful for little more than support. The elephant inherited its cumbersome legs from the mammoth. An elephant can't stand on three legs and scratch its back with the fourth, like a lion or tiger. It can't use its legs to get food into its mouth, either. Such stubby, chubby legs prevent an elephant from doing knee-bends to reach food close to the ground. The elephant's trunk makes up for the clumsiness of its legs. The trunk is an extension of its nose and upper lip and serves the elephant as arm, hand, fingers, nose and lips. The trunk is strong enough to uproot a tree, and supple and sensitive enough to pick up a single peanut or grain of popcorn. With it, an elephant can squirt water down its own throat, after first sucking it up through tubes in its trunk. (A full-grown elephant can drink about 50 gallons of water a day, which is enough to fill 200 quart milk bottles.) Without a trunk, the elephant would be quite helpless.

How did the giraffe get its long neck?

Skeletons of ancient giraffes show that once they had short necks. Then a chance jumbling of genes, which are the chemical building blocks that determine the inherited characteristics of each living thing, created a species of longer-necked giraffes. Scientists call this kind of accidental happening a *mutation.* With its long neck, the new type of giraffe was able to reach leaves higher in the trees and get more to eat than its short-necked relatives. It could also see further and escape more easily from distant dangers. This longer-necked giraffe grew in number and the short-necked one gradually died out.

Modern man got his highly developed brain in the same way. A mutation in early man created some human beings with bigger brains, and this new man was better equipped to survive and prosper. Over hundreds of thousands of years, the bigger-brained families of man outlived the smaller-brained species. Mutations occur daily among living things, but it is impossible to predict their importance until thousands of years have passed.

How can you tell frogs and toads apart?

Basically, frogs and toads are similar. Both belong to the class of animals called *amphibia*—cold-blooded animals that can live on land as well as in water—and they resemble each other, particularly when you don't see them side by side. But there are differences in their skin and in their shape. As a rule, frogs are smooth-skinned and slippery, while toads are dry and bumpy. Frogs are long and lithe, and toads squat and pudgy. There is an old superstition that if you pick up a toad you will get warts, but it is not true.

What is the biggest bird?

The world's biggest bird is the ostrich. It can weigh as much as 200 pounds and grow to be eight feet tall. Its wings are not powerful enough to enable its heavy body to fly, but the ostrich has strong legs and can run as fast as 40 miles an hour.

Why do skunks smell?

A skunk uses his smell as a defense against an enemy or when he is frightened. Under his tail he has two powerful scent glands filled with a strong-smelling fluid. Each gland has five or six sprays which the skunk can shoot singly or together. The skunk can aim this spray and fire it nine feet or more. You can tell when a skunk is about to spray because it will paw the ground or raise its tail. By that time, it is probably too late to escape. The spray can sting the eyes and certainly makes it hard to breathe. When the scent glands are removed, a skunk makes a nice, friendly pet.

What is the fastest animal?

A cheetah can run faster than any other land animal: a mile in less than one minute. In the bird world, the peregrine falcon, also known as a duck hawk, is the fastest in flight. It can speed three miles in a single minute.

Why do we need bugs?

Insects may seem like pests, but actually they are very useful. They maintain the balance of nature by feeding on other insects or providing food for them and for plants, birds and animals. By doing this, insects help regulate and support the earth's plant and animal life. The bug that eats garden vegetables may be food for a bird that destroys other harmful insects. Insects also provide needed food for marsh plants and help fertilize the soil. Some insects carry plant seeds from place to place. Bees manufacture honey and pollinate the flowers so they bloom each year. Shellac comes from an insect found in India. Silk is made by an infant insect, the silkworm. Fireflies are still used for light in Africa. Insects have been on earth for about 350 million years, much longer than man. There are more than a million known insects, more than all other species of the animal family put together, with possibly millions more still awaiting discovery. The biggest insect, the giant walking stick, may be more than a foot long. The smallest beetle could hide beneath a grain of salt.

How can a fly walk upside down on the ceiling without falling off?

On the underside of a fly's six legs are feet which have two claws. Beneath these claws are sticky pads which work like the suction cup on a rubber-tipped arrow. When the fly wants to use these suction cups, he stops walking on tiptoe as he usually does and puts his foot down. The suction creates a temporary vacuum under the claw, and this keeps the fly stuck to the wall or ceiling until he lifts his foot to make his next step.

Why do mosquito bites itch?

Only female mosquitos bite. They have a slim tube at the front of their heads which can both pierce the skin and suck blood through a hollow center. As the mosquito bites, the sucking tube takes in blood and injects a poisonous liquid into the tiny wound. This poison causes an immediate irritation and swelling. The swelling produces an itch. When you scratch, the wound swells further and itches even more.

Why does a moth eat my sweater?

Moths do not eat clothes at all. They only lay eggs on them. They are particularly fond of wool sweaters, coats, rugs and furs as nesting places. After about a week, the eggs hatch into baby caterpillars. They are the ones who eat the wool. Once the caterpillar becomes a moth, it can no longer chew anything. Its mouth is suitable only for sucking.

How does the firefly turn itself on and off?

A firefly is one of many living things that gives off its own light. It is called *luminous* because of this. Certain shrimp, fish and even a mushroom have the same ability. The firefly's body produces two mysterious substances called *luciferin* and *luciferase*. When these combine with the oxygen in the air, the firefly's light goes on. Scientists can produce this same light when they borrow the two substances from a firefly. A firefly's light gives off no heat. It is on the firefly's abdomen and keeps working, as far as science knows, for the firefly's whole life.

What does horsepower mean?

The term "horsepower" indicates the amount of power the engine of a car or any other kind of engine can produce. Before man invented mechanical engines, he always used horses for work—to turn the wheels of grain mills or pull heavy loads. When engines came into use, they replaced the horse because they could do much more work than a horse. The best way to describe the amount of power an engine had was to compare it to the power of four, or eight, or 12 horses, and so the word horsepower came into existence.

How does gasoline make a car go?

A lighted match placed near gasoline will cause the gasoline to burst into flame. This happens because gasoline combines very easily with oxygen when heat is applied. Gasoline that is close to any fire, particularly in an enclosed area, will unite immediately and explosively with oxygen. This explosive quality, called *combustibility,* is what makes a gasoline engine in an automobile work. Gasoline is turned from liquid into vapor in the carburetor of an engine, then travels to a closed cylinder where an electric spark from the spark plugs ignites it. The explosion which results in that small space pushes down a piston which in turn drives a rod that turns the car's wheels.

Who owns the roads?

Roads, in most cases, are public property, open to anyone using them lawfully. There are roads owned by towns, built chiefly to accommodate residents. There are roads owned by states, built to help citizens of all parts of a state reach each other quickly and safely. And there are roads that are interstate highways, connecting many parts of the country and built by the various states and the United States Government together. Americans pay their share of the cost of road building through taxes and tolls.

How does toothpaste get inside tubes?

Toothpaste and other kinds of tubes already closed at the top are filled in the factory from the wide bottom end, then are sealed at the bottom by machine. Some model ships get into bottles in a similar way. The man who builds model ships cuts off the bottom end of a bottle with a glass-cutting tool. Then he puts the boat inside through the wide bottom and cements the bottom back in place.

Why do telephone poles have numbers on them?

Many of the poles that line our streets and country roads are not telephone poles at all but are owned by the power company that provides your house with electricity. But all the poles have their own number so that a repairman for the company can discover which power line leads to your house. Both the power company and telephone company have charts showing exactly what wires and cables are carried by each pole. The repairman finds the number of your pole. Then he knows exactly what lines to check in order to fix the trouble.

Why does wood float?

A piece of wood floats in water because it weighs less than the same volume of water. If you can picture an amount of water shaped exactly like the piece of wood, that is, having the same volume, and if you could weigh both the wood and the water, you would find that the water would weigh more. By the laws of gravitation, the heavier thing will be on the bottom. Therefore, wood will stay on the surface when you put it in water. Wood weighs less than water by volume because it has much more air in it. The air gives it *buoyancy:* the lightness to stay afloat.

How can an iron ship float?

A block of iron sinks in water because it is much heavier than the block of water it pushes out of the way. A ship made of iron (or steel) is built so that there is a great deal of air between the bottom and its high, widely separated sides. Steel has such great strength that a ship's sides can be made in reasonably thin sections. These do not have a great deal of weight compared to the amount of air that is held between the two sides. It is the air contained between its steel sides that keeps the ship afloat.

How can a submarine go under the water and come up again?

A submarine has both an inner and an outer steel body, separated from each other by considerable air space. It can travel on the surface of the water like other ships but it can also pump out air from between the inner and outer hulls. As it does this, the air is replaced by water. The submarine, becoming heavier, sinks under the surface. The submarine can rise by reversing the process—pumping out sea water and replacing it with air, thus increasing its buoyancy.

What are shells made of?

A shell—whether seashell, nutshell, eggshell, turtle shell or any other kind—is the hard outside covering of a living thing. Its purpose is to protect what is inside. The turtle is born with a shell, and it grows with the turtle all its life. Crabs and beetles produce their own shells as they grow. They even shed their shells from time to time: as they outgrow their old shell, a soft new shell begins to form underneath it. The shells of snails are secreted by the snail and built up coil after coil as it grows. Sometimes shells are one piece, like the shell chickens and birds produce to protect their eggs. Sometimes they are two-piece: the clam and the oyster have such shells which they open for breathing and eating and close for protection.

Shells are made of many substances. The shell of a nut is made of *lignin*, a wood-like material. Seashells are made of lime or *silica*, a substance contained in glass. The shells of crabs and beetles start out as a soft material that stretches, like skin. In time this changes into a hard covering.

Why do soap bubbles break?

When we blow soap bubbles, we put air inside a skin of water, or water with soap mixed in. Because the air trapped within presses equally hard all over the inside surface of the bubble, the bubble takes the shape of a sphere, or ball. A bubble breaks because the stickiness of the soap only temporarily stops the water from flowing toward the bottom of the bubble. Eventually the wall of the bubble becomes so thin that the pressure of air inside makes the bubble burst.

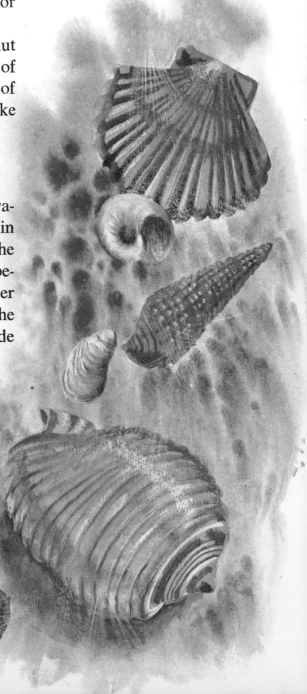

What makes the waves at the beach?

Waves at the seashore are caused in part by the wind and in part by the tide. The wind helps to get a wave started by moving the water. If there is a wind and the tide is coming in, the waves will be higher than they would be if there were the same wind and a tide that was going out. The wind and the tide work together to push the oncoming wave. Waves are also affected by the sea bottom. A beach that has a smooth, sandy bottom and slopes gradually will usually have gently lapping waves. A beach that has a rocky, uneven bottom, creating shallow water in one place and deep water in another, will produce giant breakers with the help of wind and tide.

Where does the water go at low tide?

Tides are caused by the pull of the sun and the moon on the earth's surface. Since the moon is much closer, its effect on tides is more important. When the moon is directly overhead, it actually pulls the water that is nearest it slightly away from the ocean bottom. This is what causes the tide to rise. As the moon passes over the horizon, the pull lessens and the water settles back toward the ocean floor. In most places, the water level rises a few feet at high tide and falls a few feet at low tide.

There are high tides on opposite sides of the globe at the same time. This is so because the moon's pull is least strong on the side of the world farthest away from the moon. There the water bulges away from the moon, much as if it were trying to fall into space. For this reason there are two high tides every 24 hours: one when the moon is nearest a body of water and one when it is farthest away.

Is there still buried treasure anywhere?

Though pirates no longer sail the seas, the world is still full of treasure. Most of it has nothing to do with pirates, though there are many places where pirate treasure is supposed to be hidden. Captain Kidd, for example, is rumored to have buried much of his stolen treasure on the Thimble Islands, in Long Island Sound off Connecticut. Treasure often results when ships sink in storms, accidents and war.

Other treasures lie buried in attics, beneath floorboards of houses and under the ground—the property of secretive owners who did not trust banks or their own families. Every day the newspapers report the discovery of long-hidden treasures: old manuscripts, letters, stamps and money. Many a treasure has been in full view for years, until someone comes along and realizes its worth. This is true of numberless art works discovered in attics or in antique shops.

How did people know their way when there were
no roads and maps to tell them were to go?

The North Star is almost directly above the North Pole and so it is always in the same place in the sky as the earth turns. Early man used the North Star as a guide, at least in lands north of the equator (the North Star is not visible south of the equator). Man also found his way by making his own paths and remembering them. As soon as he had somewhere new to go, he made a road by trampling down brush and breaking twigs. Early man never traveled very far, or if he did, he never wanted to find his way back to where he started. Cavemen had no permanent homes. They moved with the food supply.

The first known maps—drawn on clay tablets—were found in Egypt and are more than 4,000 years old. More elaborate maps began to be made during the third century B.C. when man started to explore the sea and travel great distances to trade.

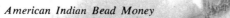

54

American Indian Bead Money

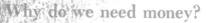

Why do we need money?

Early man did not need money. The caveman found food, clothing and shelter by himself, or he lived in a small group that shared the necessities of life. When men began to trade with one another, however, the need arose for some way to measure the value of different goods. The first such measure was not coins. In early farming societies, like Egypt, cows, sheep or grain were used as "money" because they had an accepted value for the men who were trading. At different times, salt, tobacco leaves and silver have also been used as money. Coins came into common use during the time of the Roman Empire but were used even earlier in various places.

Societies need money only when they have reached a certain stage of development. In the American colonies, many settlers did not use money. Traders carried knives and beads to exchange with the Indians for furs and other goods. A man could exchange two good beaver skins for five pecks of corn or ten pounds of pork. This was called bartering. As societies get bigger and more complicated, however, it is not so easy or convenient for a man to locate a person who wants what he has to trade. For this reason, societies adopt a means of exchange that has commonly accepted value.

What is freedom?

If you had absolute freedom to do what you liked, there would be no rules saying "you can't do this, you mustn't do that." But if one man can do anything he likes, he may interfere with another man's freedom. If a man feels he is free to pick flowers from a second man's garden, then the second man is not free to enjoy all the flowers he grows. So freedom has come to mean the right to do as you like so long as you do not harm another man or prevent him from having the same right.

Freedom cannot exist in a society that lacks choices. For instance, when there is only one piece left in a box of chocolates, it may not be one that you like. In a country where there is only one candidate for president, the citizens are not free to choose their leader. In those nations where freedom exists, a man can choose the job he will work at, live where he likes and say what he wants if he does not interfere with other men's freedom.

Roman Coin

Why are some people rich and others poor?

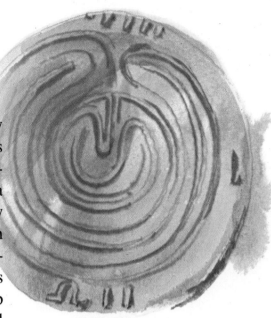

Cretan Coin

In the days of the caveman, a man who was strong usually had more possessions than one who was weak. But other forces also could affect a prehistoric man's fortune. Suppose, for example, that a small, weak caveman found an excellent cave near a mountain stream. Every day wild animals would pass on their way to get water. Without leaving the safety of his cave, this man might be able to kill many animals. There might be another caveman who was not particularly strong, lucky or clever, but who was adventurous. He might decide to leave the place where his group had always lived and journey to a distant place where hunting and fishing would be better and there he would prosper.

Civilization makes life more complicated. Some men today are born richer in the natural abilities that count in a society. Some inherit more wealth. Others live where there is greater opportunity to go to good schools and get good jobs. Still others may be at a disadvantage because of laws or customs in a society that place them in an inferior position. Those with fewer advantages have to work harder, but they may still not be able to overcome their disadvantage. Good health, good luck, intelligence, the faith and courage to seek out new opportunities and the ability to do well those things a society needs done all contribute to making a man richer than his neighbors.

Aztec Hatchet Money

Why do we need laws and policemen?

Laws are designed to protect people. Even a small family must have rules. Sometimes the rules will protect your rights: your brother cannot move things on your desk without asking permission. Sometimes the rules will spell out your obligations: you cannot go out to play until you have made your bed. Laws do the same things in a society. They state the rights and the obligations of each individual as part of a society that has millions of individuals. A law forbidding robbery helps to protect you from having your money taken by someone who may be stronger than you or threaten you with a weapon. You have a right not to be robbed. In the same way, the law forbids you to rob your neighbor, and it is your obligation as a citizen to obey the law. Laws are made so that each person can live in a group harmoniously, without fear of being harmed by others. The mother who enforces her rules and the policeman who enforces the laws are both protecting the rights of all the members of a group.

56

Hippocrates

How do we know that germs exist when we can't see them?

In ancient times, the causes of sickness were a deep mystery. Men thought illness was caused by evil spirits, since no one could understand why a person who was healthy yesterday should be sick today. In the late 17th century, the *microscope* was perfected. Through the use of a special glass, a *lens,* which made once invisible things visible, man soon discovered a whole new world of tiny, one-celled animals and plants—germs—that had never been seen with the eye alone. The plant form of germs was called *bacteria,* the animal form, *protozoa.* Later, still a third form, impossible to see with an ordinary microscope, was found and named *viruses.*

How does the doctor know a medicine will make me better?

Like all other skills men practice, medicine is based on knowledge and experience gathered from the time the profession began. In ancient Greece, Hippocrates studied the science and art of healing and wrote down what was known up to that time. Since then, doctors have tried many different herbs, tonics, salves, ground mineral compounds (pills) and, most recently, antibiotics, to cure infections and disease. As they have learned more about the workings of the human body and the causes of many illnesses, they have been able to give medicines in the form of vaccines which can stop us from getting some sicknesses in the first place. Past medical experience, sound medical training and new scientific experiments all help your doctor to know which medicine is likely to make you better. And today's doctor has a great deal of help. Medical researchers, biologists and chemists, using powerful electronic equipment, make new discoveries about the body and about germs. Drug manufacturers try to develop new and better medicines. When you get better with the help of a medicine, you become an example that a particular cure really works.

How do X rays "see" inside you?

In 1895, a German scientist named Wilhelm Roentgen discovered that when an electric current is passed through a glass bulb from which most of the air has been removed, a ray something like light is produced. It is not light, because the ray cannot be seen by the eye. For lack of a better name, he called it X (meaning unknown) ray. X rays can penetrate many substances that light won't go through. X rays pass easily through vegetable matter and the flesh of animals, but not through more brittle materials like glass, minerals, metals and human bones. When a doctor takes an X ray picture, the rays pass through the flesh making pale shadows on a film plate. Bones or swallowed objects like a safety pin make heavier shadows, since the X ray penetrates them only slightly, if at all. When the film is developed, a doctor can tell by looking at these shadows that a bone is broken or a penny is where it shouldn't be inside a person's body.

What are tonsils?

There are actually four pairs of tonsils in your nose and throat area, but the most visible ones are those at the back of your throat called *pallatine* tonsils. Tonsils are masses of *lymphoid* tissue, responsible for the production of *lymphocytes,* the germ fighters in your bloodstream. Scientists think that tonsils probably help to trap infectious germs before they can enter your body. Tonsils do not have to be removed unless they repeatedly become infected. Then they are a danger to health. Once tonsils are removed, there are many *lymph nodes,* located throughout the body, that can continue to produce the much-needed lymphocytes.

58

How can scientists know how old the earth is?

If written history is just 5,000 years old, how can man know what happened billions of years ago? One way is through the *fossils* (hardened remains) of animals and plants preserved in the earth. Then, too, cave dwellers in later times left crude weapons, utensils and other remains. Most important, the earth itself tells scientists about times past. The earth was built in layers. The earliest rocks were formed from the earth's molten hot core. These are the *basalt* rocks that hardened to make the foundations of our continents and the floors of our oceans. Scientists now can date the origin of the earth as a planet from 4,530,000,000 years ago—give or take 40 million years. They arrived at this figure by computing the amounts of lead and uranium in a basalt rock sample taken from deep inside the earth. Their analysis was based on the rate of decay of these elements.

This technique can now be applied to anything that once lived on the earth—animal or vegetable. By computing the rate of decay of carbon 14, a radioactive element which exists in all living things and which slowly destroys itself in dead things, scientists can determine the exact age of any remains.

When did the first man who looked like us arrive on earth?

The oldest bones of a human type are at least 400,000 years old. But the first men on earth who are thought to be our true ancestors were those who arrived after the end of the Ice Age about 15,000 years ago. At this time, two types of human beings appeared called *Cro-Magnon* and *Combe-Capelle*. In size, brain capacity and both head and chin structure they were almost like us. (We know this from skeletal remains found in caves in south-central France.) While anthropologists agree that these two types of human being are part of our ancestry, there were certainly other men who existed then and from whom we are descended.

Head of the Egyptian King, Ramses·II

Where do mountains come from?

Mountains look so big, so important and immovable that we may think they have been where they are since the beginning of time. This is not true. All mountains were made by violent explosions and changes in the earth's surface that happened, in most cases, millions of years ago. They came into existence in one of four ways, or a combination of them. There are *folded mountains,* created when great pressure under the earth's surface squeezed layer upon layer of rock up in large, uneven folds. The European Alps are an example. There are *domed mountains,* formed when melted rock pushed up great, rounded blisters in the earth's surface. The Black Hills of South Dakota are such mountains. *Faulted mountains* came into being when inner pressure caused breaks in the earth's crust, and pushed huge blocks of rock above the surface. An example is the Sierras in the western United States. Finally, there are *cone-shaped mountains,* which have craters in their tops. These were caused by volcanic eruption. Mount Vesuvius in Italy and Mount Fujiyama in Japan are examples of this kind of mountain. Mountain ranges were formed over long periods of time when one or more of these violent changes occurred.

What is a volcano?

A volcano is an opening in the earth's crust caused by a violent explosion of gases and liquid rock. When melted rock spreads in areas deep under the surface of the earth, it concentrates in weak spots where cracks or spaces exist. As the melted rock pushes in, the gases in these open spaces are crowded together. Over a period of time, if there is enough pressure, the gases will explode through the crust of the earth creating a volcano and bringing up large quantities of ash and liquid rock.

What is an atom?

When science knows the full answer to this question, many other puzzling questions about the universe may be answered, too. The word *atom* comes from the Greek and means "not divisible." In ancient times, the atom was thought to be the smallest possible bit of any substance. Today scientists have found that an atom of any element has more than 20 different particles in it. Some of them are *electrons, protons, neutrons, positrons, neutrinos, mesons, hyperons.* These particles move at very high speeds around and within the central core. How they are held together is still unknown. At the present time we know of about 100 different kinds of substances, or *elements,* such as gold, oxygen, iron and so on. An atom is the smallest possible part of an element. All of the atoms of any one element are just alike, but atoms of different elements are never alike.

Where do rocks come from?

There are three different kinds of rock. One kind, called *igneous,* was formed in prehistoric times from the liquid matter of the earth's fiery core. Basalt and granite are such rocks. A second kind, called *sedimentary,* was created when water, wind, ice and violent storms worked on ancient decaying vegetable and animal matter so that these materials were subject to great pressure and turned to stone. Such rocks formed in layers and are called *stratified.* Sandstone and limestone are of this sort. The third kind—*metamorphic* rock—was once one of the other two. Over long periods of time, this rock was subjected to further pressure or heat, or both, and changed into something else. Marble is rock of this sort. All of these different kinds of rock are composed of one or more minerals. Uranium, iron, copper and other minerals, called *ores,* can be removed from rocks.

Is there life on other planets?

Within our solar system, scientists discount the possibility of life on any of the nine planets, with the possible exception of Venus and Mars. These are the two planets nearest earth. Their temperatures are not too extreme, and they are thought to have both water and an atmosphere, two requirements for life. In recent years astronomers have begun to consider the possibility that life exists on other planets circling some of the older stars in our galaxy. Many of these stars are larger than our sun, and billions of years older. They might well have the right temperature to nourish life. If this is so, scientists feel that life on these older planets may be far in advance of our own. While it seems unlikely that we could ever travel across the trillions of miles separating us from these planets, some astronomers feel that radio communication with such distant worlds may be possible.

If we live on the outside circle of the earth, why don't we fall off?

Every object exerts a pull called *gravitation* on every other object. This pull is determined by the weight of the objects and by their distance apart. The earth is so much heavier than anything else on it that it pulls us all toward itself with enormous force. We are held down to it every minute of the day. Whenever we move, we must exert our own muscular force to counteract the great force of the earth's gravity. (This is what tires us in physical activity.) But try as we will, we can never exert a muscular force that will let us rise off the earth. This is not the case on the moon. The moon is much smaller than the earth and so the pull of its gravity is only about one sixth as strong. With every step a man took on the moon, he would find himself rising several feet in the air.

If you hear apples mentioned in connection with the laws of gravity, it is because Isaac Newton, who was a 17th-century English mathematician, first guessed at the probable causes and rules of gravity while watching apples fall from trees.

Why do stars twinkle?

The light that shines down from the stars is steady. But when this light passes through moving layers of air at different temperatures, its rays are bent at various angles. This bending makes the stars seem to twinkle.

Why isn't the moon always whole like the sun?

The sun is always round and shining because its glowing gas flames give off a constant light. The moon is a cold, dead planet which does not give off any light of its own. It can be seen from the earth only because it reflects some of the sunlight it receives. The moon travels around the earth every 28 days. During this time, the moon always has one full half lit by sunlight. But that half faces the earth only once in the moon's trip around the earth. If you hold a tennis ball directly in front of you and stand with your back to the sun, you will be in the position of the earth (with the ball as your moon) at the time of the full moon. If you then turn to your left, you will see that the tennis ball (moon) is soon only half-lit. When you have come around halfway and are facing the sun, you will see that this is when the moon cannot be seen at all. The side of the moon away from the earth is then lit by the sun, the side facing the earth is in shadow, and there is no sunlight for the moon to reflect toward the earth. That is why there is a full moon only once every 28 days.

What is a falling star?

A falling star is really a sky pebble—a *meteor*. These small stone-like bodies, made of iron or other minerals, travel through space, generally in swarms of thousands. They are bits of matter which break away from distant stars. If some of these pebbles enter our atmosphere, they fall with such speed that they burn up on entering the earth's atmosphere, leaving a trail of burning gas, which we call a "falling star."

Where do the stars go in the daytime?

The stars we see in the night sky shine just as brightly by day. Like the sun, stars are glowing-hot masses of gas. Those we are able to see with the naked eye are, in fact, much bigger and brighter than the sun. But the sun is 93,000,000 miles from earth and the nearest star is 25,000,000,000,000 (25 trillion) miles away, or 25 million times as far. Because the sun is much closer, its light appears so bright to our eyes during the day that it completely blots out the glow of the brighter but more distant stars.

If the world is round, why does it look flat?

The world looks flat because of its great size in relation to us. If you were to lay a toothpick on a basketball, it would touch the ball for about one-quarter of an inch, giving the impression of flatness for that space. Since the earth is some 44 million times the size of a basketball, it appears flat as far as any human being's eye can see.

How big is outer space?

If you left today on the fastest rocket that science has yet devised, you would not reach the sun until a year from now. It would take you 33 years to reach the orbit of the smallest and most distant planet in our own solar system, Pluto. Beyond that, there are about 100 billion stars in our own galaxy, the Milky Way, and the nearest of these would take thousands of years to reach. Beyond our galaxy, there are billions of other galaxies, each with billions of stars. All of space with everything in it is called the universe. Though scientists know many things today that were undreamed of even 25 years ago, we still do not know just how much space there is, or if it is measurable.